THE HISTORY OF THE WORLD

Written by
Christopher Maynard, Philippa Moyle
and Paul Harrison

Designed by
Chrissie Sloan

Illustrated by
Kim Woolley

zigzag

About this book

The world hasn't always been the same as it is today. This book tells you about the people and events that have made history over thousands of years.

Find out how people have travelled on land, water and in air. Discover how the way people dress has changed over the years. These and many other fascinating topics are explored in clear text and colourful illustrations.

The illustrated Timeline that runs through the book shows you the developments and inventions that have changed the world from earliest times to the present day.

AD 1050 Sailors in Europe find their way using astrolabes.

AD 1065 Stained glass is fitted in the windows of Augsburg Cathedral in Germany.

AD 1066 A huge comet appears. It is later called Halley's Comet.

AD 1066 William the Conqueror becomes King of England.

AD 1086 The Domesday Book is completed.

This book was created and produced by Zigzag Publishing Ltd, The Barn, Randolph's Farm, Hurstpierpoint, Sussex BN6 9EL, England

Consultants: Richard Tames & Chris Nichols
Richard Tames is a freelance writer, specialising in history. He has written many books for children as well as contributions to encyclopedias.
Chris Nichols is Head of History at Patcham High School, Brighton, Sussex.

Cover Illustrator: Peter Bull
Editors: Philippa Moyle & Paul Harrison
Senior Editor: Nicola Wright
Editorial Director: Colin Shelbourn
Design Manager: Kate Buxton
Assistant Designer: Deborah Chadwick
Production: Zoë Fawcett
Series Concept: Tony Potter

Colour separations by ScanTrans, Singapore
Printed by New Interlitho, Italy

First published in 1994 by Zigzag Publishing Ltd

ISBN 1 85993 024 7

10 9 8 7 6 5 4 3 2

Contents

Words and writing

Although people have been talking to each other ever since they lived in caves, we have no idea what the first language was like. However, there are very good records of what people said when they finally began to write things down.

Languages

There are about 4,000 languages spoken in the world today. Only about a hundred of them are widely spoken. Many languages are spoken by small groups of people. There are about 50,000 Aborigines in Australia who speak several hundred different languages.

The alphabet

The word alphabet comes from the first two letters of the Greek alphabet - 'alpha' and 'beta'.

Some of the letters that we use today are over 2,500 years old. To begin with, the Ancient Romans had only 23 letters in their alphabet. Later, in the Middle Ages, the letter 'i' was divided into 'i' and 'j', and the letter 'v' into 'u', 'v' and 'w', making a total of 26 letters.

English

The first king of England to speak a modern form of English most of the time was Henry IV. He became king in 1399. Before this, English kings spoke mostly French because of William the Conqueror. He left France in 1066, attacked England, and became King William I. He spoke French, as did the English kings after him, until Henry IV.

Pencils

Graphite mines were discovered in Cumbria in 1564. A year later, Konrad Gesner, in Germany, placed a piece of graphite inside a metal holder and used it to write on paper. This was the first pencil with a lead made of graphite.

Ballpoint pens

Ballpoint pens are filled with ink that dries very quickly. The first ballpoint pen was invented in 1938 by Lazlo Biro, a Hungarian journalist. People used his surname for ballpoint pens and they became known as 'biros'.

Printing

In 1454, a German printer called Johann Gutenberg invented a printing press. Each letter of the alphabet was individually made in metal which meant that it could be used over and over again. The letters were put together to form words. In 1455, he produced the first printed Bible on his printing press.

The first page of Gutenberg's Bible

8000 BC People start to grow crops. The first known farming town is Jericho.

7000 BC Clay pots are used for storing food and drink.

6000 BC The fibres of plants and the fleece of sheep and goats are used to make clothing.

6000 BC Bricks are used for building.

5000 BC People dig irrigation ditches from rivers to water their crops.

4500 BC People fish with hooks in the Black Sea.

Ink

About 2,500 years ago, the Chinese invented ink. They used to burn oil in their lamps which left behind soot. They then mixed this soot with water and glue to make ink. They used the ink for writing.

Picture writing

The first form of writing was done around 3200 BC by the Sumerians who lived in Mesopotamia (now called Iraq). They drew pictures of goods that they had bought and sold on clay tablets. Over the next 200 years, they invented a pattern of symbols which were etched on to soft clay with a reed. This type of writing was called 'cuneiform' which means wedge-shaped.

A Sumerian clay tablet

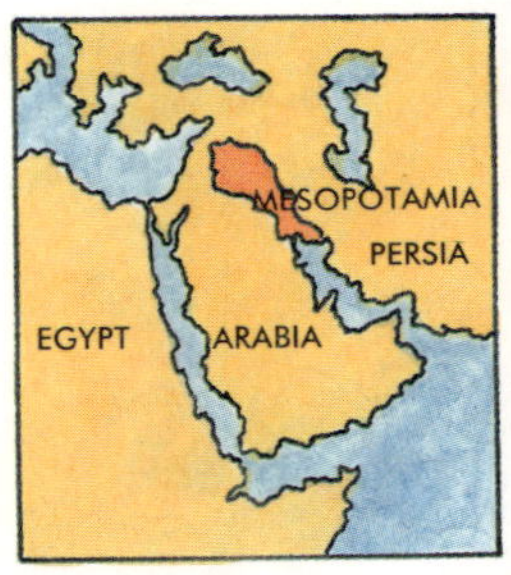

Newspapers

The first newspaper to be published daily appeared in Germany in the 1620s. It was known as the Leipzig Journal, and was published regularly until 1918.

Hieroglyphics

The Ancient Egyptians invented their own type of picture writing, called 'hieroglyphics'. Like cuneiform, each symbol represented one sound. About 2600 BC, the Egyptians began to write on sheets of papyrus, a kind of paper made from papyrus reed.

Chinese writing

The Ancient Chinese also invented a form of picture writing between 1523 BC and 1027 BC. Each of the symbols, called characters, represented an object. The Ancient Chinese used brushes instead of reeds for their writing.

Today, the Chinese still write in characters. They start at the top of the page and work down in columns.

3600 BC Tin is mixed with copper to make bronze. It makes better tools and weapons.

3200 BC Picture writing appears in Mesopotamia.

3200 BC Carts are fitted with solid wooden wheels in Mesopotamia.

3000 BC The Egyptians use cloth to make clothes.

3000 BC A board game is played in Mesopotamia.

2000 BC People in Egypt use shadow clocks to tell the time.

Farming

In the past, farming was mostly done by hand. Today, farmers use many different machines to plant and harvest crops. They also use machines for milking cows and shearing sheep.

The first farmers

About 10,000 years ago in 8000 BC, people began to grow crops along the River Nile in Egypt, and the Rivers Tigris and Euphrates in Mesopotamia. These people were the first farmers.

The farmers used wooden hoes and simple ploughs to prepare the ground for sowing the seed. They harvested the crops using small hand-held sickles with blades made of sharpened flints. They grew wheat and barley, and kept goats, sheep, pigs and cattle.

Ploughs

The wooden ploughs used by the first farmers had a pointed end which dug into the soil. The farmer guided the plough using its two handles. At first, the ploughs were dragged across the ground by hand. Later, they were pulled by oxen.

An early plough

About AD 600, a new plough was invented by the Slavs of Eastern Europe. This plough could cut heavy, wet soil. It turned the soil over as well as cutting it, allowing the water to drain away. This formed the basic design for the modern plough.

1500 BC The Hittites of Turkey heat ore with wood to make iron.

1300 BC The first alphabet, with each letter as a single sound, appears in Syria.

1000 BC Scissors made of bronze are used in Asia.

700 BC In Mesopotamia, concrete is made to build a canal.

700 BC The King of Lydia, in Ancient Greece, makes the first coins.

510 BC The first known map of the world is drawn by a Greek mapmaker.

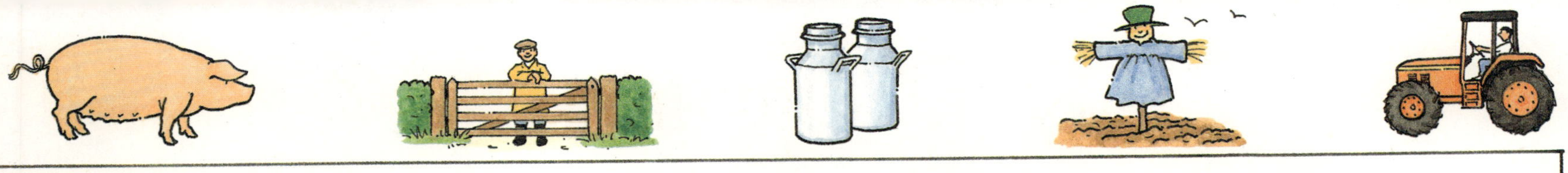

Dogs

Dogs began to live with people about 12,000 years ago, around 10,000 BC. It is likely that dogs started looking for scraps of food around people's homes. After a time, they moved in and settled down.

People found dogs to be very good workers, as well as good company. They helped to hunt animals and were excellent at herding sheep and goats.

Insect killers

About 2,000 years ago, the Ancient Chinese invented a chemical that killed insects. They mixed a poison with chrysanthemum leaves to make a powder that killed fleas. However, the first really powerful insect-killing chemical was DDT. It was discovered around the time of the Second World War. Although it was very good at killing insects, DDT also killed birds, fish and other animals. Today, it is banned in most parts of the world.

Windmills

The first windmills appeared in Persia (now called Iran) about AD 700. However, they only became common in Northern Europe in the 1100s. They were fitted with sails that turned a heavy stone quickly. This ground grain into flour.

A few hundred years later, windmills were also being used to pump water. In Holland, they helped to drain marshy ground, so it could be used for farming.

A windmill from about 1180

Fertilizers

People have been using animal manure on fields to help crops grow for thousands of years. Chemical fertilizers were first invented in 1840 by an Irishman called James Murray. He mixed bones with sulphuric acid and put it on crops. The result was amazing as fields produced huge harvests of crops.

Barbed wire

In 1874, Joseph Gliden from the USA invented a machine that could make barbed wire by the mile. This cheap fencing was used to divide the American West into farmland within a few years.

500 BC The quill pen is made from a sharpened feather.

350 BC The Romans begin to build roads from one end of their empire to the other.

300 BC Pulleys are used for lifting heavy objects.

285 BC The first lighthouse is built off the coast of Egypt.

100 BC The Romans invent central heating for houses.

70 BC The Romans use water-wheels to grind grain and crush olives to make oil.

Eating and drinking

Five hundred years ago, in the 1400s, nobody had ever heard of hamburgers or pizzas. As for chips, people in Europe didn't even know what a potato was! Potatoes were only introduced to Europe in the 1560s from South America.

A meal in the Middle Ages

Eating in the Middle Ages

The Middle Ages lasted from about the 1100s to the 1500s. During this time, people mainly ate with their fingers. They used a knife for cutting up meat and a spoon for eating soup, but there were no forks. They helped themselves to food from the serving dishes with their hands.

The Italians began to use forks in the 1500s. Before this, they were only used in the Middle East. For a long time forks were a luxury, used only by kings and nobles. It wasn't until the 1700s that they became commonly used.

AD 50 Soap is used by the Romans as medicine.

AD 105 Papermaking is invented by the Chinaman Tsai Lun.

AD 271 The first compass is used in China.

AD 300 Chinese riders use stirrups so they can stand up on their horses.

AD 475 Horses in China use collars so they can pull heavy loads.

AD 500 Tea is brought from India to China.

Tin cans

The first company to pack food into tin cans was set up in 1812 in Blue Anchor Lane in London. Its owners had learned how to make tin cans from a French inventor two years earlier. They knew that heating food inside a sealed can would kill off any germs, so that the food would not spoil.

Meals on wheels

In the USA in 1863, a restaurant car that served hot meals was added to the train that ran from Baltimore to Philadelphia. It was an immediate success.

Mustard

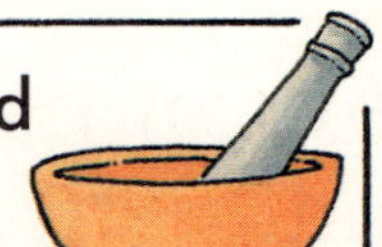

When the Gauls of France attacked Ancient Rome in 390 BC, they took some seeds with them. They crushed the seeds and mixed them with grape juice, called must. The result was a hot-tasting paste which the Romans called *mustum ardeo*. Today, we call it mustard.

Microwave ovens

Dr Percy Spencer

A scientist called Percy Spencer found that when he left a bag of corn cobs near an electronic tube, called a magnetron, they turned into popcorn. The corn cobs were cooked by radio waves from the magnetron.

The idea of cooking with radio waves was developed. In 1952, the first microwave ovens went on sale in America. They were made out of bits and pieces from radar sets used during the Second World War.

Chocolate

The first people to enjoy chocolate were the Aztecs, who settled in Mexico in the 1200s. They made a chocolate drink from cocoa beans which they picked from cacao trees.

Spanish explorers took this chocolate drink to Europe in the 1500s, where it soon became very popular. It was not until 300 years later, in 1819, that people in Switzerland ate chocolate in hard bars.

Coffee

When coffee was first introduced to England in the 1650s, many people thought it

could cure all kinds of illness. Advertisements for coffee claimed that it was good for coughs, colds, headaches and sore eyes, and that it helped indigestion.

An early microwave

AD 550 Early forms of chess are played in India.

AD 600 The Slavs of Eastern Europe invent a plough which can cut heavy soil.

AD 700 The first windmill appears in Persia.

AD 700 Mills driven by water-wheels are used in Europe.

AD 748 Printed newspapers appear in China.

AD 750 Beds become common in France and Germany.

Making a home

A house doesn't need to have running water, lights, central heating and a fitted kitchen to be a comfortable home. In the past, people have lived happily in homes ranging from tents to igloos.

Living in caves

Between 35,000 and 85,000 years ago, people called Neanderthals made their homes in caves all over Europe. The caves had areas for sleeping and cooking. There was also an area for cutting up the meat of the animals they caught.

The cave dwellers lit a fire at the entrance to the cave. They used it to cook their food, and to keep them warm. It was also useful for frightening off wild animals.

Mud bricks

About 8,000 years ago, people who lived in Egypt, Israel and Mesopotamia made bricks from clay. They left them in the sun to harden. The clay bricks were used to build houses. However, heavy rain could turn the bricks to mud.

About 5,500 years ago, people began to bake bricks in ovens, called kilns. This made the bricks hard and waterproof. The oldest known bricks came from the town of Jericho.

Roof doors

Çatal Hüyük in Turkey is the oldest town yet discovered. Here, people lived in one-room houses made of mud bricks. Inside each house there were benches and platforms along the walls where people sat, slept and worked. Rush mats covered the dirt floor. The door was a hole in the roof!

The houses were packed together so tightly that there was no room for any streets. People walked along the roofs, using ladders to get from one roof to the next.

AD 760 Arabic numbers, the ones we use today, appear in Baghdad.

AD 765 Picture books are printed by hand in Japan.

AD 770 Horseshoes are used in Europe, allowing horses to travel further.

AD 802 The first rose trees are planted in Europe.

AD 850 An Ethiopian goatherd discovers coffee berries.

AD 868 The first written book, *The Diamond Sutra*, is printed in China.

Thatched roofs

From 500 BC, people called the Celts settled in Britain, France, Germany, Spain, Italy and Holland. They built their homes out of woven branches, and plastered clay over the gaps to keep out the wind and rain. The roofs were made of thick layers of thatch. These protected the house from the rain and kept in the warmth.

Moving homes

In the 1100s, the Mongols travelled through Central Asia. They lived in tents, called yurts. Yurts had a light wooden frame which was covered with sheets of felt. The sheets were covered with animal fat to make them waterproof - it was very smelly inside! Yurts could be put up or taken down within a few hours. They could be moved about on carts pulled by oxen.

Wooden houses

The Vikings lived in long, wooden houses. Inside, there was a single room where all the family ate, cooked and slept. A hole in the roof let out the smoke from the fire. In winter, animals often moved indoors and lived at one end of the house. They helped to keep it warm.

AD 900 Nobles begin to live in castles all over Europe.

AD 942 Good quality wool and linen cloths are made in Flanders.

AD 950 The Chinese use gunpowder for fireworks.

AD 963 London Bridge is rebuilt across the River Thames. It is made of wood. Later ones, like this, were made of brick.

AD 969 Playing cards are used in China.

AD 996 Cane sugar arrives in Europe from Egypt.

Dressing up

People have been dressing up, putting on make-up and wearing perfume for many thousands of years. These things have become part of everyday life.

Buttons

When buttons were first made, they were used as jewellery to decorate clothes. It wasn't until the buttonhole was invented in the Middle Ages that buttons were used to fasten clothes.

Umbrellas

Umbrellas were invented by the Chinese about 11 BC. For a long time they were used to shade people from the sun instead of to keep off the rain.

In Europe in the 1700s, only women used umbrellas as a way of staying dry. Then Jonas Hanway, who was English, started to use an umbrella. At first, men laughed at him, but gradually the habit of using an umbrella became popular with men.

Ties

In Ancient Rome, soldiers often wore bits of fabric round their necks when they dressed up. Later, in the 1600s, Croat soldiers in the French army wore brightly coloured neck-bands. These later became known as cravats, which are like ties.

Today, it is popular for men to wear a jacket and tie. Children also wear ties for special occasions.

Bras

In Ancient Rome, female gymnasts wore a scarf over their breasts to give them support. This was the first bra.

Perfumes

In Ancient Greece and Rome, rich people wore scented ointments to make them smell nice. The scent of these ointments was made by soaking leaves, flowers and roots in oils or animal fats.

Shoes

Tens of thousands of years ago, when people still lived in caves and huts, they wore shoes and boots made of pieces of animal skin stitched together. About 6,000 years ago, in Ancient Egypt, people wore shoes made out of papyrus reed.

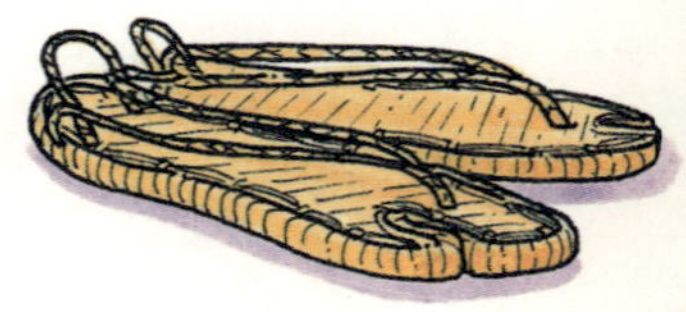

The habit of making right shoes different from left shoes only began about 1,000 years ago. Shoes were made to fit people's feet individually. It is only in the last 100 years that shoes have been made in factories in standard sizes.

AD 1050 Sailors in Europe find their way using astrolabes.

AD 1065 Stained glass is fitted in the windows of Augsburg Cathedral in Germany.

AD 1066 A huge comet appears. It is later called Halley's Comet.

AD 1066 William the Conqueror becomes King of England.

AD 1086 The Domesday Book is completed.

AD 1090 A mechanical clock, driven by water, is built in Peking.

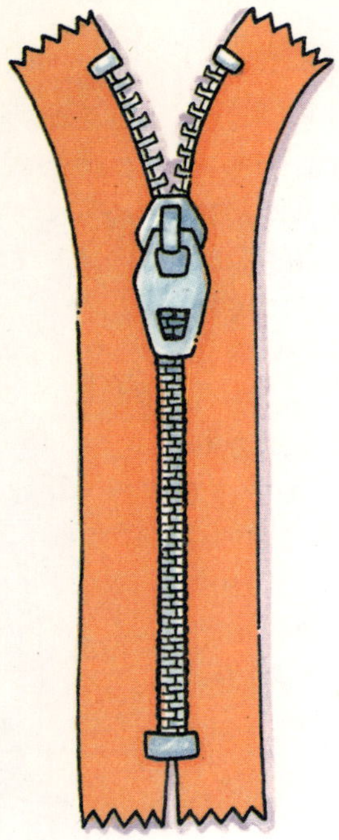

Zips

In 1913, a Swedish-American engineer called Gideon Sundback, designed the modern metal zip. Five years later, the US Navy ordered 10,000 zips as fasteners for flying suits. The name 'zip' comes from the sound the slider makes as it opens and closes.

Make-up

In Ancient Egypt, rich women wore make-up. Cleopatra, who was a beautiful Egyptian queen in the first century BC, used a bright green paste of copper minerals as eye shadow. She also painted her eyebrows and eyelashes with black kohl. Kohl was a cream made out of sheep's fat and a powdered mineral of lead. She used ochre, which was a clay stained red with iron, as lipstick. She also painted the palms of her hands with henna, a red-brown dye, to make them look young.

Cleopatra applying her make-up

Jeans

About 1850, a tailor in San Francisco called Levi Strauss began making trousers for local miners from tough tent cloth. They were called jeans, were hard-wearing and well made. Today, Levi's jeans are still extremely popular.

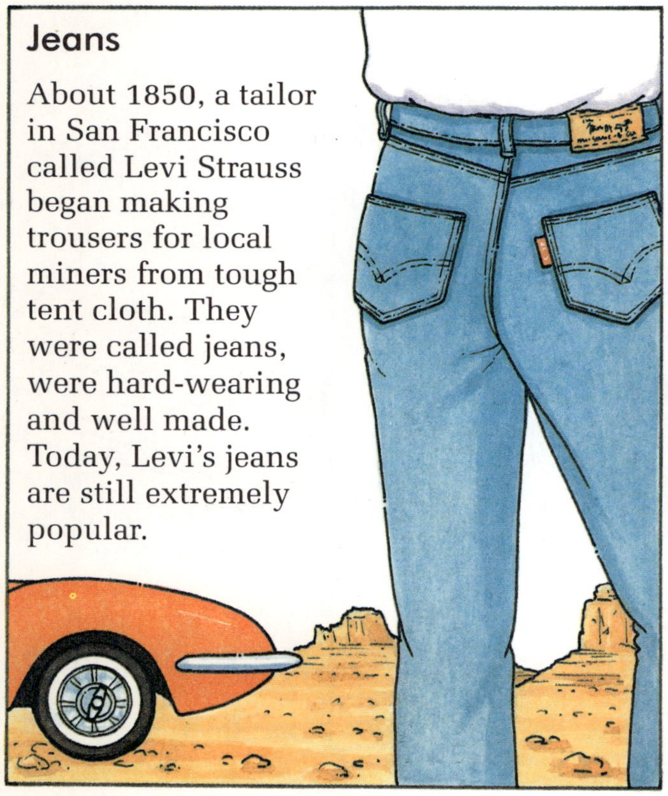

AD 1094 Gondolas are used as water taxis in Venice, Italy.

AD 1100 The Chinese print paper money using multicolour printing.

AD 1100 The University of Bologna is set up - the first university in Europe.

AD 1180 The first windmills with sails are built in Europe.

AD 1191 The Japanese learn to drink tea from the Chinese.

AD 1200 People begin to wear engagement rings.

Getting better

People have been visiting doctors for thousands of years. Sometimes, their treatments worked, but often the cures were worse than the illness itself!

Anaesthetics

For many years, surgery was a horrible experience for patients. Surgeons would operate while their patients were still wide awake! The introduction of an anaesthetic, called ether, made a huge difference. A patient would breathe in this gas before an operation, and become unconscious. The surgeon could then work without the patient feeling any pain.

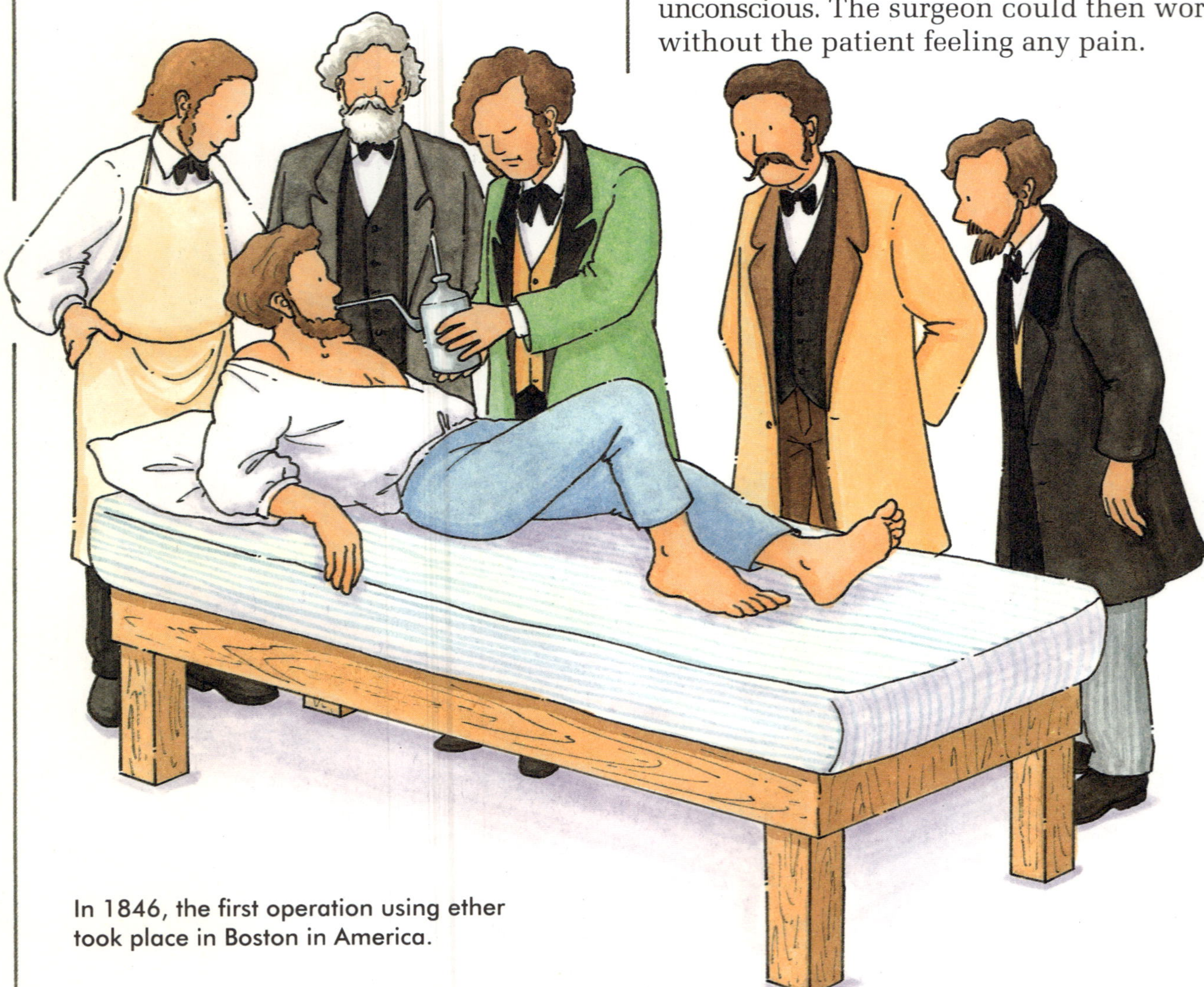

In 1846, the first operation using ether took place in Boston in America.

Tea

In China, tea wasn't only something you drank to relax. It was an important medicine as well. It was given to people as a laxative. This is a medicine that helps people to go to the toilet regularly.

Transplants

A transplant is when an organ, like a heart, is moved from one person to another.

The first organ to be transplanted was a kidney in 1950. In 1967, the first heart transplant was carried out in South Africa.

AD 1212 Work starts on Rheims Cathedral, in France.

AD 1215 King John signs the Magna Carta in England.

AD 1225 Cotton cloth is made in Spain.

AD 1232 The Chinese use kites to send messages during battles.

AD 1233 Coal is mined near Newcastle in England.

AD 1271 The explorer, Marco Polo, sets out on his overland journey to China.

Leeches

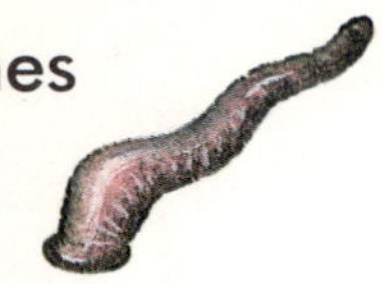

In the past, one of the most popular ways of draining poisons out of a patient was by blood-letting. Doctors placed blood-sucking leeches on their patient's skin to suck out the poison.

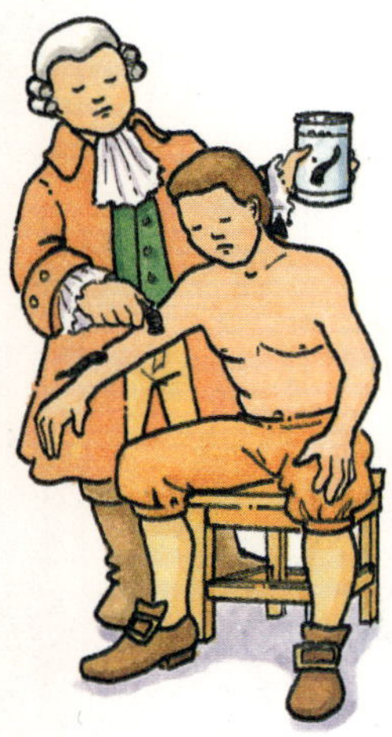

The Romans used blood-sucking leeches about 2,200 years ago. The practice continued all over Europe for many hundreds of years until this century.

X-rays

An X-ray machine uses an invisible beam to take pictures of the bones inside a human body. X-rays can pass through skin and flesh, but not through bones. The first X-ray picture of the human body was taken in 1895.

The Black Death

A plague was a disease that killed lots of people. The worst ever plague was the Black Death of the 1300s. It killed about a quarter of all the people in Europe. People had no idea what caused it. In Rome, they lit fires in the street to try and stop it from spreading. They thought that this would kill any poisons that were floating in the air. Now we know that the disease was actually carried by rat fleas.

Thermometers

In 1612, an Italian doctor called Santorio Santorio used the water-filled thermometer invented by Galileo, in 1593, to measure human body temperature.

Spectacles

In 1290, an Italian called Salvino degli Armati invented a pair of eyeglasses which made objects look bigger. These were the first spectacles.

AD 1278 Glass mirrors are invented.

AD 1285 Florence is the biggest business centre in Europe.

AD 1290 Spectacles are invented.

AD 1308 An indoor tennis court is built in Paris.

AD 1347 The Black Death kills a quarter of the people in Europe.

AD 1368 Rebuilding work begins on the Great Wall of China.

Cleaning

Today, soap and toothbrushes are found in every home but, two hundred years ago, people couldn't afford these everyday objects as they were thought to be luxuries. Now we have washing machines and vacuum cleaners which make it far easier to keep our clothes and homes clean.

Roman baths

The Romans were very keen on taking a daily bath. As well as bathing at home, they went to large public baths, where they washed, chatted and passed the time of day.

You can still see the remains of Roman baths in the city of Bath in England.

Toothbrushes

The Ancient Chinese were the first people to use toothbrushes. By about 1650, they began to be used in Europe, too. In 1780, the first model with a handle and bristles, like the toothbrush we use today, was invented.

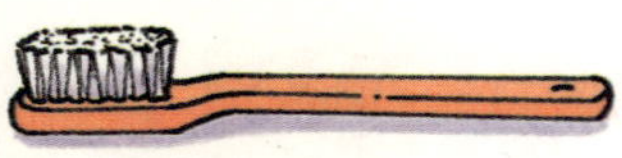

Toothbrushes with nylon tufts were first made in the USA in 1938.

Flush toilets

The first known flush toilet was designed by Sir John Harrington in 1589 for his new house near Bath. It had a tank of water for flushing and it drained into a pit beneath his house. However, the idea did not catch on.

Almost 200 years passed before the flush toilet became popular. Alexander Cummings invented the first widely used toilet in 1775. By 1870, toilets had S-bends with water in them to keep out the smell of the drains.

A decorated Victorian toilet

AD 1400 Blast furnaces are used to make cast iron.

AD 1405 Metal screws are invented.

AD 1415 Jan van Eyck discovers how to use oil paints.

AD 1455 Johann Gutenberg produces the first printed Bible.

AD 1464 A royal mail service is started in France by King Louis XI.

AD 1490 Leonardo da Vinci invents the parachute.

Soap

People only learned how to make soap in hard bars around the year 1200. Soap remained an expensive luxury until late in the 1700s when Marseilles soap began to be made in large quantities.

Vacuum cleaner

Hubert Booth invented the first vacuum cleaner in 1901. His machine sat on a trolley that was pulled up and down the street. The machine stayed in the street while someone went from house to house, cleaning the dirt out of people's carpets with a long hose. William Henry Hoover manufactured a vacuum cleaner around 1908. Hoover machines became very famous and are widely used today.

An early Hoover

Washing machines

The first washing machine was made in 1782. It was a wooden tub filled with hot soapy water. In the 1800s, machines had a mangle above the tub. This was used to squeeze water out of the washed clothes.

In 1907, Alva Fisher of America built the first electric washing machine. This had a motor which turned a drum containing the clothes. The sort of washing machines we use today appeared in 1960.

An early washing machine with mangle

AD 1490 Orphanages for children whose parents have died are opened in Italy.

AD 1490 The first ballets are performed for noblemen in Italy.

AD 1492 Christopher Columbus lands in the Bahamas, America, thinking he is in China.

AD 1492 Leonardo da Vinci draws plans for a flying machine.

AD 1497 Vasco da Gama sails around the southern tip of Africa on his way to India.

AD 1504 The first pocket watch is made in Germany.

Working

Today, many people work in offices and shops but, two hundred years ago, most people worked on the land. The Industrial Revolution began with the invention of new machines. People left the countryside to look for work in the factories and mills that were being built.

Craftspeople

In the Middle Ages, all goods were handmade. In towns, they were made by skilled craftspeople who had spent years learning their trade. From about 1300, all craftspeople were obliged to join guilds. A guild set standards of quality and prices, and made sure that all new craftspeople were properly trained. There were guilds for masons, candlemakers, glassmakers, tailors, shoemakers and dozens of other trades.

Farming

In the 1700s, great changes took place in the way people farmed. New crops were grown, and better animals were raised. Machines that could work much faster than people began to be invented.

For thousands of years, seed was sown by people scattering it over the ground by hand. This was a wasteful and expensive process. In 1701, Jethro Tull invented a horse-drawn seed drill that could plant three rows of seeds at the same time. With the new seed drill, he used only a third as much seed as before, but the amount of wheat grown in an acre nearly doubled.

Jethro Tull's horse-drawn seed drill

Steam power

Machines powered by steam engines began to be used in farming in the 1800s. This threshing machine, dating from 1860, was used to strip grain from the stalk. It could do the work of a whole team of people.

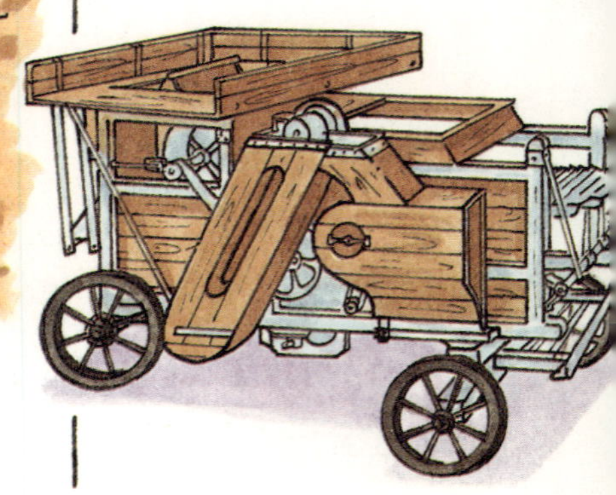

AD 1504 The pocket handkerchief is first used.

AD 1506 The first loads of spices are brought to Europe by sea from the East Indies.

AD 1509 Wallpaper is printed in England. At first it comes only in black and white.

AD 1517 Coffee is drunk in Istanbul for the first time.

AD 1540 Wooden legs are fitted to the limbs of wounded soldiers.

AD 1543 Copernicus describes how the Earth circles around the Sun.

Mill work

During the early 1800s, thousands of people in Britain began to work in mills that made cotton and woollen cloth. The mills had rows of steam-driven machines that spun and wove cloth much faster, and more cheaply, than anyone could by hand.

The mill owners employed women and children as they could pay them less than men. The women and children worked long hours and were badly treated. The machines they used were dirty, noisy and dangerous - there were often accidents.

Modern factories

Cars have been built on long assembly lines in factories for most of this century. An assembly line is where things are made in stages, moving from one stage to the next to get different parts added, until they are complete. Today, many parts of the assembly line use robots. They are especially good at doing dangerous or dirty jobs such as welding and painting.

AD 1559 The first European encyclopedia is written.

AD 1564 Lead pencils are made using wood and graphite.

AD 1589 William Lee invents the first knitting machine.

AD 1589 Flush toilets with underground sewage tanks are designed.

AD 1590 A microscope is invented in Holland.

AD 1593 Galileo invents the glass thermometer.

Learning

Until the 1800s, most children were not given the opportunity to learn how to read or write. Before this, only the children from wealthy families were educated. They were often sent to boarding schools, or had private tutors at home.

Schools

Over 4,000 years ago, wealthy Sumerians in Mesopotamia sent their children to school to study reading, writing and arithmetic. In those days, only boys were allowed to go to school. They read their lessons out loud, and used damp clay tablets to practise their writing. Teachers were very strict with them. A pupil might be beaten if he did not do his work correctly.

Universities

The first people to set up places of higher education were the Arabs. In AD 971, a university opened in the city of Cairo in Egypt.

The first university in Europe was set up at Bologna in Italy. It began to take students in 1100. The students went there to train as monks and priests. They had come from monastery schools, but were educated to a much higher level at the university. For a long time, all university teachers were men of the Church.

AD 1600 The recorder becomes popular.

AD 1605 The first newspaper appears in Antwerp in Belgium.

AD 1607 The first English settlement is made at Jamestown, Virginia, in North America.

AD 1608 Cheques are used to pay bills for the first time in Holland.

AD 1609 The Dutch East India company ships tea from China to Europe.

AD 1619 African slaves arrive in North America.

American education

The Europeans who settled in America in the 1600s were keen to educate their children. They passed laws that forced all parents to make sure their children learned to read.

Sailing school

Prince Henry of Portugal was so interested in the idea of exploring the coast of Africa that he set up a school of navigation at Sagres. Expedition leaders, pilots and mapmakers went there from all over Europe to plan expeditions, design better ships and learn how to navigate.

From Sagres, Henry sent dozens of expeditions south to sail along the coast of Africa. In doing so, they overcame the fear of falling off the edge of a flat Earth or being boiled in hot seas at the Equator. Due to a keen interest in his school and sailing, he earned the nickname 'Prince Henry the Navigator'.

Free schools

In England, in the 1800s, laws were passed that made it illegal to keep a child out of class. Free schools were set up everywhere, so that even the poorest children could be educated. This was the start of the school system that we know today.

A university was set up in Paris 30 years after Bologna. The first college in England was set up at Oxford by 1200.

Harvard College

American settlers opened Harvard College in Cambridge, Massachusetts, in 1636. It was named after John Harvard, a wealthy man who had left his library and a large sum of money to be given to a new college after his death.

AD 1625 Fire engines are used in London.

AD 1628 William Harvey discovers how blood circulates.

AD 1642 Blaise Pascal invents the first calculator.

AD 1653 The first letter boxes appear in Paris.

AD 1666 The Great Fire of London destroys much of the city.

AD 1677 In Paris, ice cream is eaten for dessert.

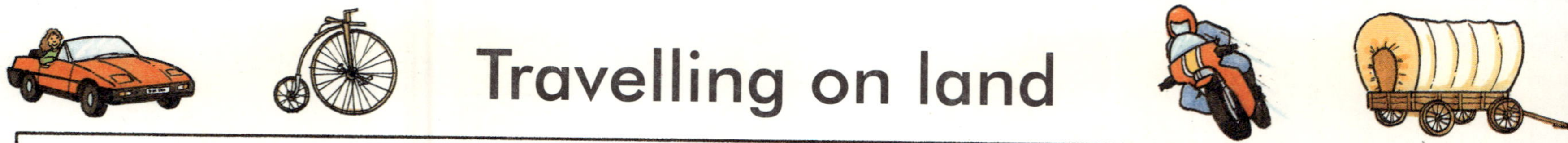

Travelling on land

It is only quite recently that people have had the benefit of rail travel or comfortable motor cars. Before cars and trains were invented, people travelled by horse and cart, or on foot.

Roads

The Romans were excellent road builders. They made long, straight highways that were paved with stone slabs, and were hump-shaped so water could drain off them. The roads were used by Roman armies to travel quickly from one area to another. The Romans built almost 50,000 miles of road, some of which can still be seen today.

Bicycles

The very first bicycles had two wheels, and were made of wood. Riders pushed along with their feet and steered with simple handlebars. These machines were called 'hobby-horses', and they were very popular from around 1819. In 1839, Kirkpatrick Macmillan added pedals to the bicycle. These turned the back wheel using a set of rods. This model was the ancestor of the modern bicycle.

Motorcycles

In 1868, two French inventors, Ernest and Pierre Michaux, fixed a small steam engine behind the seat of a bicycle. It turned the back wheel using leather belts.

Later, in 1885, Gottlieb Daimler designed a wooden motorcycle, fitted with a petrol engine. It could travel at nearly 18 km/h.

AD 1700 The clarinet is invented.

AD 1709 The first piano is built in Italy.

AD 1712 The first reliable steam engine is invented by Thomas Newcomen in England.

AD 1732 Sleeping powder is invented in England.

AD 1738 Cuckoo clocks appear in the Black Forest region of Germany.

AD 1742 The centigrade scale of temperature is used on a thermometer.

Trains

The first public railroad was the Stockton and Darlington railway. It opened in September, 1825. An engine called *Locomotion* pulled a set of open wagons. In front, a man on a horse carried a red flag to warn on-lookers.

In 1829, George Stephenson and his son Robert built an engine called *Rocket* which could travel at 56 km/h when it had no wagons to pull. It ran the first regular passenger train service from Liverpool to Manchester.

Cars

The ancestor of the car was a strange-looking steam-powered carriage, built by Nicholas Cugnot in 1770. It was heavy, very unstable to drive, and ran out of steam after fifteen minutes.

In 1885, Karl Benz built the first motor car. It was a three-wheeler with a small engine that turned the back wheels. It ran on petrol and reached speeds of 14 km/h.

Two years later, Gottlieb Daimler built the first four-wheeled car. It looked just like a horse carriage, but had an engine underneath it.

Underground trains

The first railway built to run under a city was opened in London in 1863. The trains were pulled by steam locomotives that burned coke. Before long, the insides of the tunnels became caked with soot. In 1890, electric trains began to replace the steam trains. This made underground travel much cleaner.

AD 1752 Benjamin Franklin of the United States invents the lightning conductor.

AD 1767 James Hargreaves invents the Spinning Jenny.

AD 1770 False teeth made from porcelain are used in France.

AD 1783 The Montgolfier brothers of France build the first hot-air balloon.

AD 1789 The French Revolution starts in Paris. People are executed by the guillotine.

AD 1796 A vaccine against smallpox is used by Edward Jenner in England.

Travelling on water

The first boats were made out of hollowed-out logs, or bundles of reeds. They were used for crossing rivers and lakes, but were not strong enough to sail across the sea.

Old boats

The oldest boat found so far is a dugout canoe made out of pine wood. It was made in Holland about 9,000 years ago. In England, a wooden paddle of about the same age has been discovered.

Skin tubs

About 8,000 years ago, people in Wales paddled about in tubs called coracles. They were made of wood, and covered with greased animal skins.

Sails

The Ancient Egyptians started to use sailing ships about 6,000 years ago. Their boats had a single mast and a square sail made of a reed or papyrus matting, or linen. This sail could only be used when the wind was behind the ship which is why there were oars, too. These boats were used to travel up and down the River Nile.

Fast sailing ships

The fastest cargo carriers with sails were the clippers of the 1800s. These ships were first built in the USA. They had many sails and could travel at 37 km/h on long trips, such as carrying tea from China. Clippers were so called because they 'clipped' so much time off journeys.

AD 1800 The first electric battery is made in Italy.

AD 1801 William Symington builds the first successful steamship, called *Charlotte Dundas*, in Scotland.

AD 1807 Gas lamps light up the streets of London at night.

AD 1808 The first mechanical typewriter is built.

AD 1822 Gideon Mantell finds the first dinosaur teeth.

AD 1823 Charles Macintosh of Scotland introduces the waterproof coat.

Iron ships

The first boat with an iron hull was built in 1777. Before this boat was built, people had thought that iron was too heavy to use, and that a boat made of iron would sink.

By 1843, big iron ships fitted with screw propellors, like *HMS Great Britain*, were travelling across the Atlantic Ocean.

Underwater boats

In 1624, Cornelius Drebbel tested a strange-looking submarine rowing boat in the River Thames. It had a wooden frame, and was covered with greased leather to make it waterproof. It was weighed down, so that it could float just below the surface.

It wasn't until 1900 that submarines were able to travel on the surface of the water, and dive below, using engines rather than weights. John Holland designed such a craft, which could travel 40 km under the water and 800 km on the surface.

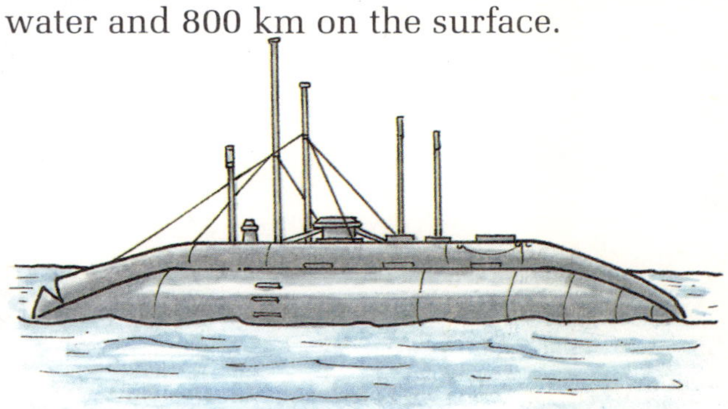

Hovercraft

The hovercraft was invented in 1955 by Christopher Cockerell. Hovercrafts float over water on a cushion of air, which is kept in place by thick fabric skirts. As they hover just above the surface of the water and don't touch it, they can also skim over flat beaches and sandbanks.

AD 1827 The first photograph is taken in France.

AD 1829 Louis Braille introduces his system of raised dots to allow blind people to read with their fingers.

AD 1829 A sewing machine is built in France.

AD 1839 The bicycle with pedals is invented.

AD 1839 Baseball is first played in America.

AD 1840 Postage stamps begin to be used on letters.

Travelling in air

People have always dreamed of being able to fly. About two thousand years ago, the Ancient Greeks told the story of Icarus, the boy who tried to fly. It was not until the 1700s that people first travelled in the air.

Airships

An airship is like a large balloon which can be steered in any direction. The first flight in an airship was made by Henri Giffard in 1852.

The most famous airships were the Zeppelins, first flown by Count von Zeppelin in 1900. They were a popular form of transport until 1937, when the airship *Hindenburg* crashed.

Hot air balloons

The first people to build a balloon were the Montgolfier brothers in 1783. They built a 15-metre high balloon from linen, and filled it with hot air. On its first test flight, Jean Pilâtre de Rozier and the Marquis d'Arlandes flew 9 km over Paris.

AD 1851 Double-decker buses are used in London.

AD 1855 David Livingstone crosses Africa and discovers the Victoria Falls.

AD 1857 The first elevator is put into a department store in America.

AD 1857 Work starts on a trans-Atlantic cable for sending telegraph messages from Europe to America.

AD 1859 Work starts on the Suez Canal.

AD 1861 Daily weather forecasts start in Britain.

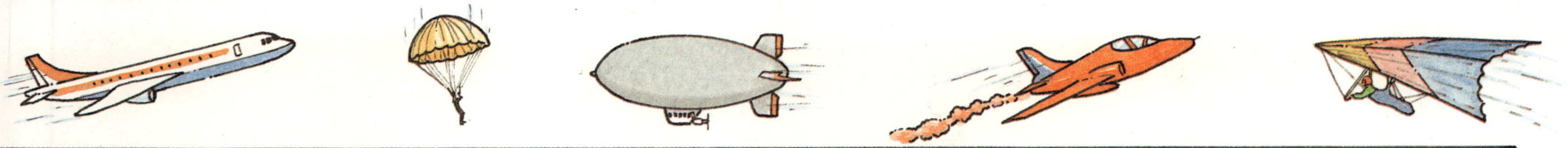

Hang gliders

The first hang glider flights were made by Otto Lilienthal in the 1890s. He invented a two-winged glider from which he hung by his arms. He steered by swinging his body about.

Jet airliners

The first jet airliner was the Comet. Its engines were placed inside the wings, rather than fixed underneath them, which is where most aeroplanes have their engines today. The Comet could carry 36 passengers and cruise at 790 km/h, nearly twice as fast as propeller planes. When it went into regular service in 1952, it changed the way people travelled around the world.

Aeroplanes with engines

In 1903, the brothers Orville and Wilbur Wright launched an aeroplane into the air from the sand dunes at Kitty Hawk on the east coast of the USA. Their two-winged aeroplane, *Flyer*, wobbled a few feet into the air, and stayed up for 12 seconds under its own power. This was the first flight by an aircraft fitted with a motor.

Concorde

Concorde is the first airliner to travel at supersonic speed, which means that it can travel faster than the speed of sound. When flying flat out, it can cruise at twice the speed of sound, which makes it the fastest passenger plane in the world. It can take 139 passengers across the Atlantic Ocean in just over three hours.

AD 1863 Roller skating becomes very popular in America.

AD 1864 The Red Cross is set up.

AD 1877 Public telephones appear in the USA.

AD 1895 The first cinema is opened by the Lumière brothers.

AD 1895 The safety razor is invented by Gillette.

AD 1896 The first modern Olympics are held in Greece.

Fighting

People have always fought each other with weapons. Over thousands of years, weapons have developed from sticks and rocks to bombs that are controlled with the help of computers.

Armour and arrows

Armour protected soldiers when they went into battle. In the Middle Ages, soldiers on horseback were covered from head to foot in complete suits of armour. The armour was so heavy that the soldiers could only get on to their horses with the help of a special lifting machine.

Although armour protected soldiers when fighting face to face, it offered little protection against bolts from crossbows and arrows from longbows. The crossbow was a popular weapon, which could kill a knight in armour from 200 metres. Longbows had a greater range, and could be fired much more quickly.

The picture below shows knights in chain mail armour fighting with swords, spears, axes and longbows.

AD 1901 A radio message is sent across the Atlantic by the Italian inventor Guglielmo Marconi.

AD 1903 The Wright brothers fly the first aeroplane.

AD 1903 The teddy bear is invented. It is named after the American President Teddy Roosevelt.

AD 1914 The First World War begins. It ends in 1918. At least 10 million people are killed.

AD 1921 Motorways are built in Germany.

AD 1922 The first film with sound is made in Germany.

Swords

Swords were first used in the Middle East around 3500 BC. These early swords were made from bronze. By 1100 BC, swords were made from iron, a much stronger metal than bronze. Swords were made in many different shapes and sizes, from large two-handed swords in the Middle Ages, to swords with narrow blades, called rapiers, in the 1700s.

Fighting with rapiers in the 1700s

Cannons

At first, cannons were little more than big, iron pots fastened on sledges of wood. They were almost impossible to aim.

One cannon, called a pot-de-fer, was used to shoot a giant arrow, but by AD 1350, it was usual to fire iron or stone balls.

Hand guns

The first guns looked like small versions of cannons. They were made from long shafts of wood with small, iron tubes fixed inside them. They were fired at the enemy by hand. At first, the guns were so heavy that soldiers firing them had to steady the barrel with a wooden stand.

Bombs

Explosives have been used in wars for hundreds of years. Bombs were thrown by hand or buried under walls. They were made bigger and more powerful as time went by.

On August 6th, 1945, the newly-invented nuclear bomb was dropped on Hiroshima in Japan. The blast killed 75,000 people and destroyed the city. Even larger bombs have now been built. There are so many that the whole planet would be destroyed if they were used.

AD 1925
A working model of a television is shown to the world.

AD 1937
The jet engine is designed.

AD 1939 The Second World War begins. It ends in 1945. Between 35 and 60 million people are killed.

AD 1940 The first helicopter flight ends safely.

AD 1942 A small nuclear reactor is tested - it works.

AD 1946
The world's first computer is built in the USA.

Inventing

Inventions can change the way we live. Over the years, people have invented thousands of different things. Some of them have turned out to be far more important than expected.

The wheel

One of the most important break-throughs was the invention of the wheel. It is thought that the wheel was first discovered about 3500 BC in Mesopotamia. The first wheels were made of planks of wood joined together.

Clocks

De'Dondi's mechanical clock of 1364

Around 1300, the first mechanical clocks, driven by weights, appeared in Europe. They could measure hours and minutes very accurately. As long as they were wound up regularly, they kept good time.

The telescope

In 1608, a Dutch maker of eyeglasses, called Hans Lippershey, held two lenses one behind the other. He found that they made far-away objects look bigger. This was the first telescope.

A year later, Galileo Galilei built a telescope that could make objects look 30 times bigger than their real size. He used it to study the planets and stars.

Galileo Galilei

Steam power

In 1712, Thomas Newcomen developed a steam engine for pumping water out of a flooded mine. It had one large piston that was moved up and down by steam. The piston drove a water pump that drained the mine. Newcomen's engine was a huge machine but, in spite of its size, it was very slow. Nevertheless, it was a success in its time.

Light bulbs

The electric light bulb was invented in 1879 by Thomas Edison. The bulb was made of glass. It only lasted for 13 hours, but its light was bright and steady.

AD 1953 Mount Everest, the world's highest mountain, is climbed.

AD 1955 The design for a hovercraft is finished.

AD 1961 Russia sends a man into space.

AD 1963 Cassette tapes are sold.

AD 1969 American astronauts land on the Moon.

AD 1971 Video cassette recorders are sold.

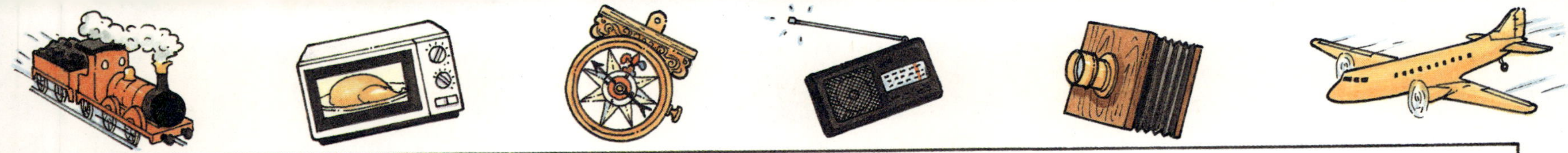

The telephone

The modern telephone was invented in 1876 by Alexander Graham Bell. Bell spilled some battery acid on himself, and called out to his friend down the speaker of the telephone, 'Mr Watson, come here, I want to see you!'. Watson, who was upstairs, heard Bell's voice through the speaker of the telephone, and ran down to see what was the matter.

Radio waves

Heinrich Hertz discovered radio waves in 1887. However, it was Guglielmo Marconi who first used them to send messages. In 1897, he radioed a tugboat that was 29 km away. Four years later, in 1901, Marconi sent a radio message from Cornwall in England to Newfoundland in Canada.

Computers

The first computer was built in 1946 in the USA. It was huge (see the timeline on page 29). In 1951, computers went on sale. They were still very large, and needed many people to run them. The first personal computers appeared in the USA in 1977. Today, computers are widely used in offices, schools and at home.

AD 1972 Pocket calculators are sold.

AD 1977 Personal computers for use at home and in the office are invented.

AD 1978 The first test-tube baby, called Louise Brown, is born.

AD 1979 Personal stereos are sold.

AD 1981 The first space shuttle, *Columbia*, is launched.

AD 1991 Virtual reality games are introduced.

Index

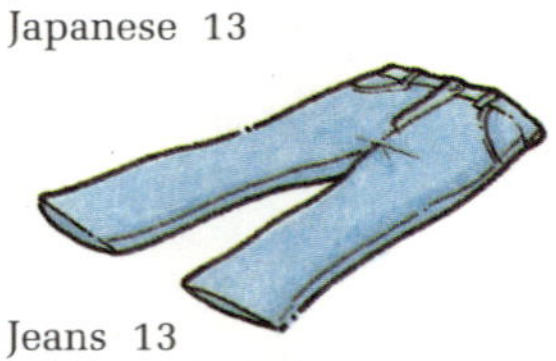